THANKSGIVING
Activity Book for Kids

The Mus
Well-Being Institute

HAPPY

THANKSGIVING

HAPPY THANKSGIVING DAY

HAPPY

THANKSGIVING

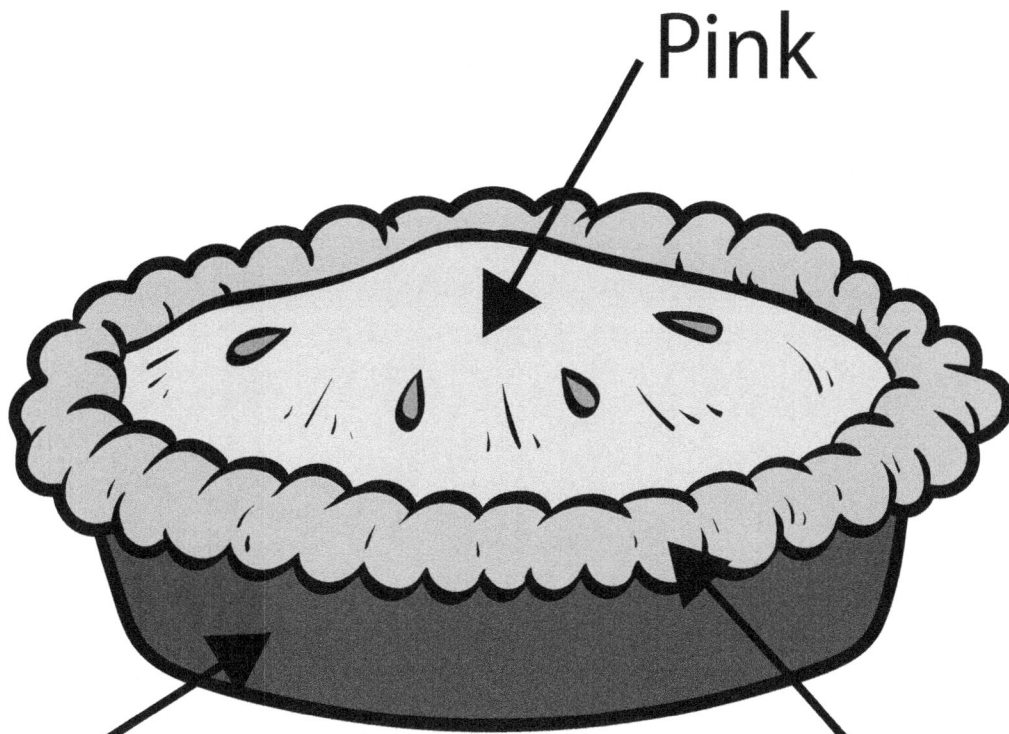

Pink

Brown

Yellow

1 - light blue   2 - gray   3 - green   4 - dark green   5 - yellow
6 - orange   7 - red   8 - brown   9 - pink 10 - black

TURKEY

LETTER SOUND
Circle the beginning sound for each picture

_urkey

W
M
T

_orn

C
S
K

_irl

H
G
R

_ie

A
E
P

THANKSGIVING WORD SEARCH

P	U	M	P	K	I	N	H	K	A
T	A	M	Y	M	E	L	A	O	C
E	T	U	R	K	E	Y	R	A	R
A	K	P	O	N	D	A	V	J	A
M	A	Y	F	L	O	W	E	R	N
P	U	M	R	M	O	N	S	I	B
I	T	O	A	I	L	E	T	S	E
L	U	P	I	L	G	R	I	M	R
G	M	I	N	A	K	M	E	B	R
M	N	N	O	P	I	E	L	E	Y

CROSSWORD
Thanksgiving day

1. **NATIVE**

WORD SEARCH CROSSWORD
Thanksgiving day

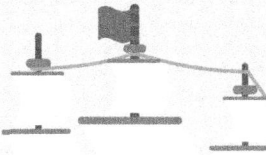

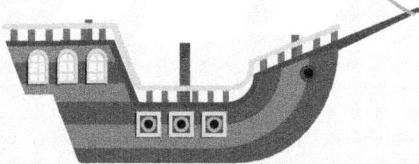

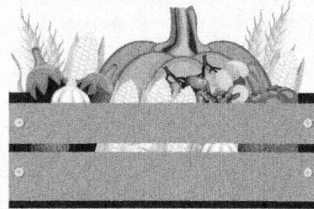

T	H	P	K	C	B	E	K	M	S
R	A	S	S	T	F	T	G	A	A
Z	T	C	W	I	K	U	W	Y	Q
P	B	A	V	H	C	R	H	F	Z
U	N	R	J	A	O	K	E	L	A
M	A	E	Z	R	R	E	A	O	C
P	T	C	Z	V	N	Y	T	W	V
K	I	R	Y	E	R	O	W	E	X
I	V	O	L	S	P	I	E	R	U
N	E	W	F	T	I	P	A	R	

NATIVE
HAT
CRANBERRIES
CORN
MAYFLOWER
PIE
TURKEY
SCARECROW
WHEAT
HARVEST
PUMPKIN

Copy the turkey

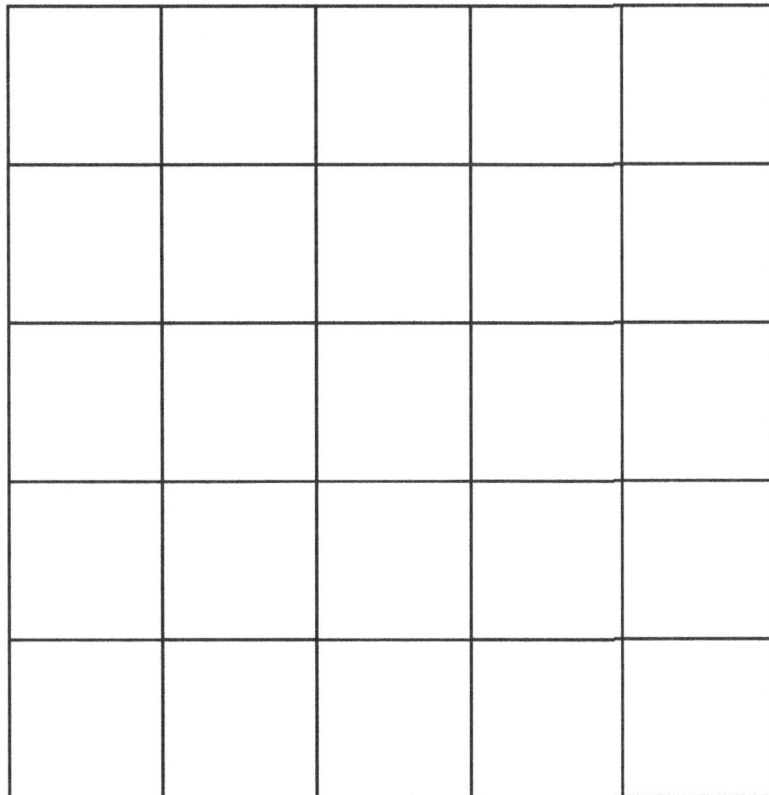

Place the letters in right order

u

r

k

y

T

e

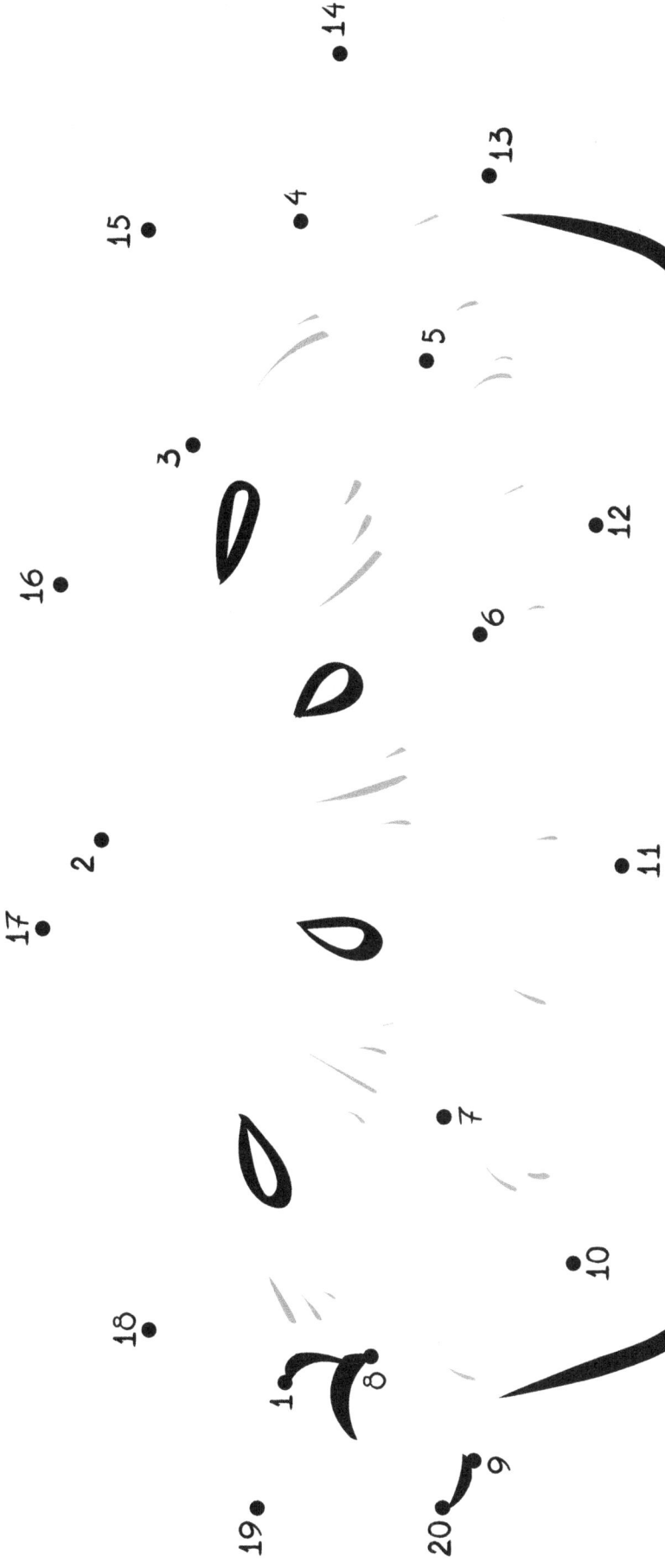

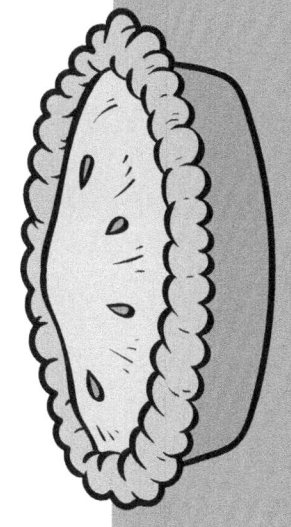

for
kids

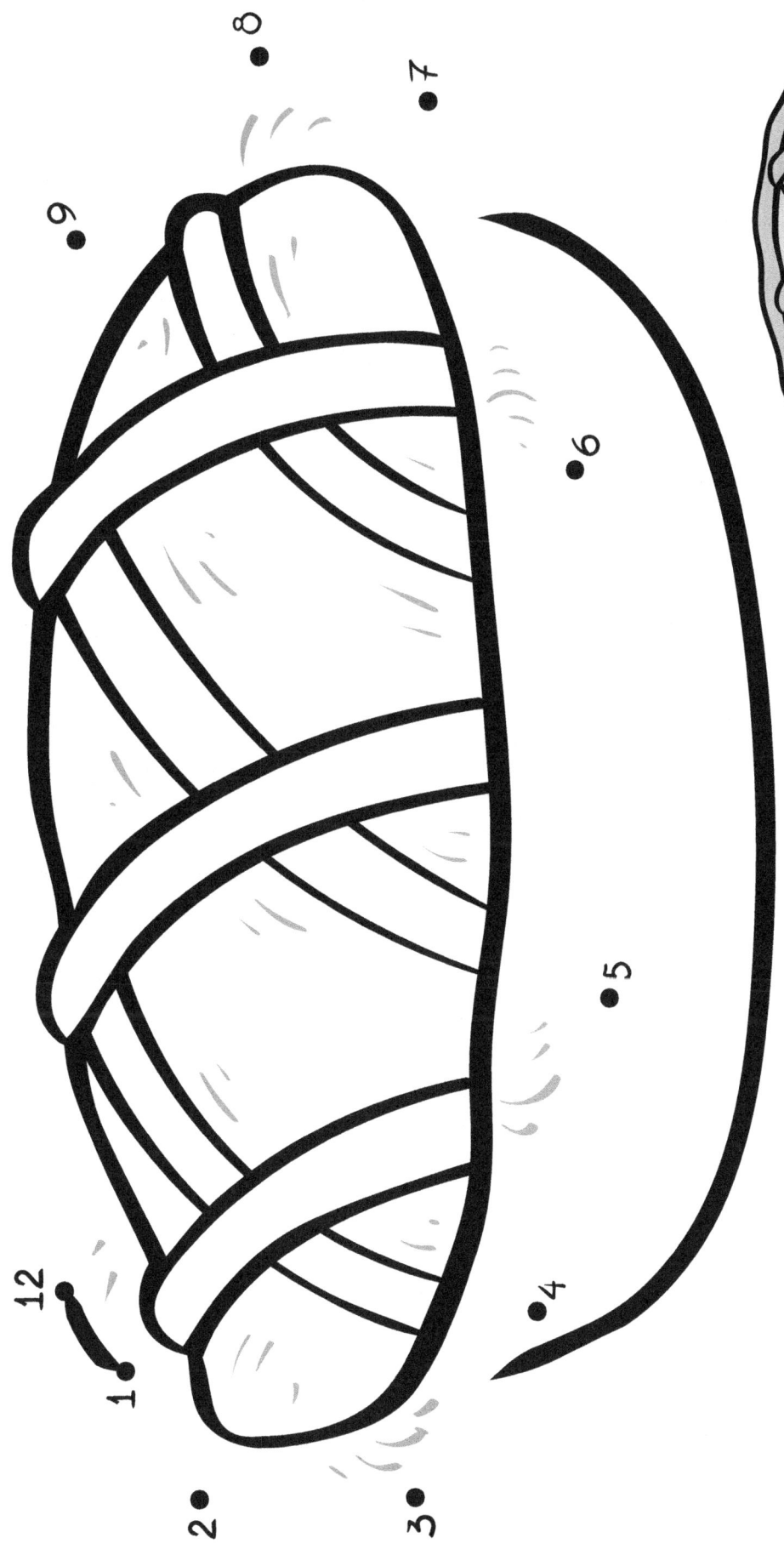

for kids

Find the ten differences

FIND
2 identical turkeys

Find the right shade!

Answer:

Happy Thanksgiving

1
2
3

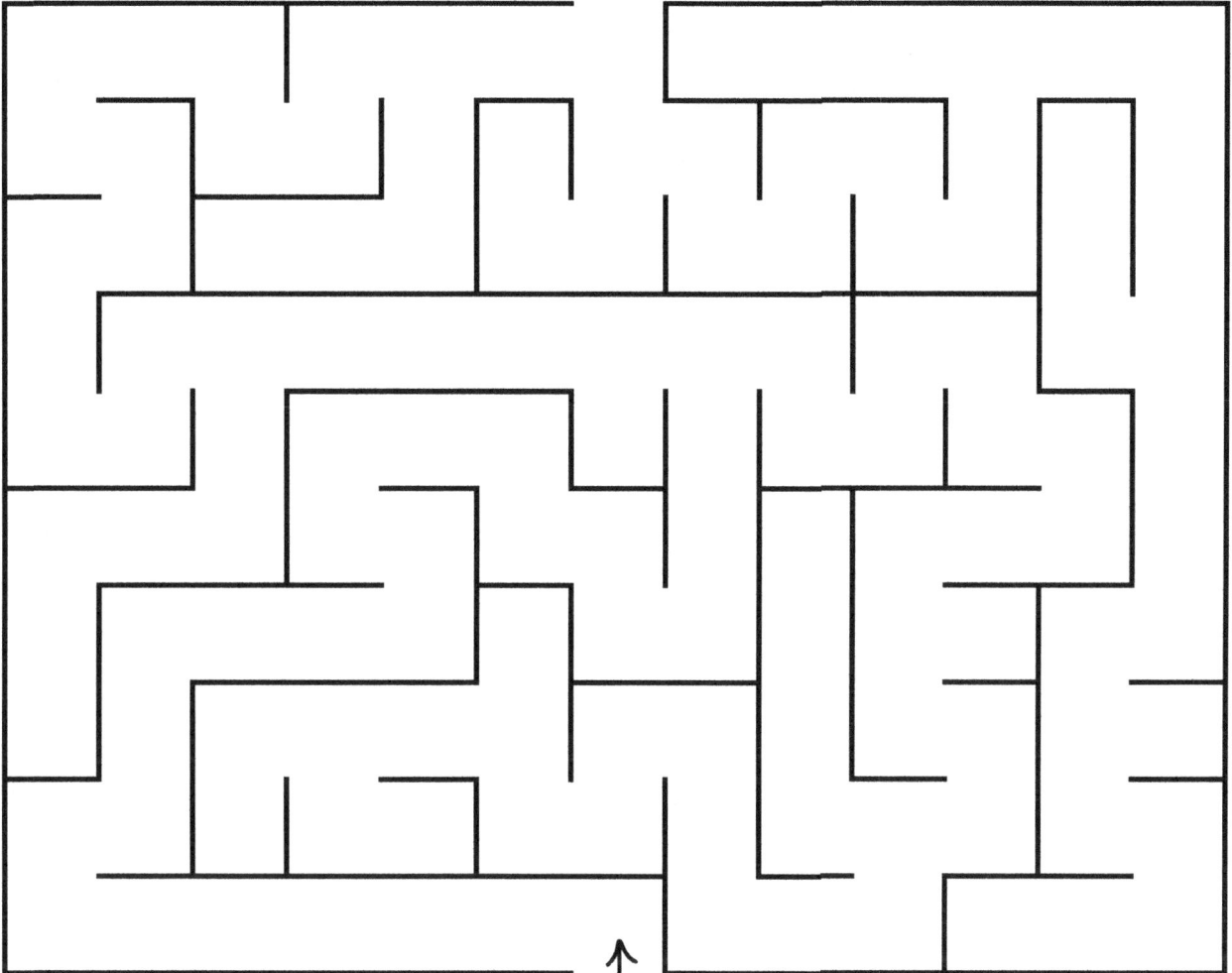

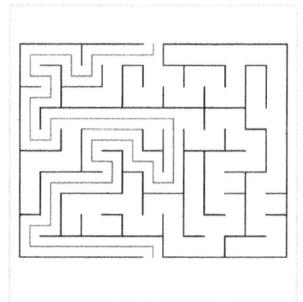

What comes next?

HOW MANY?

 ◯

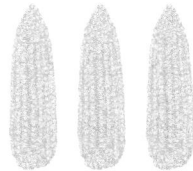 ◯

 1

2

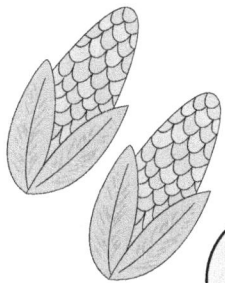 ◯

4

 ◯

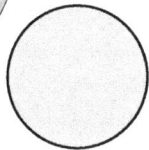 6

 ◯

5

3

 ◯

Connect numbers with a suitable number of objects

 1

2

 3

4

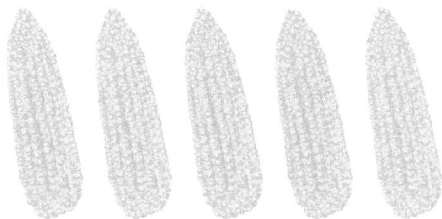 5

6

 7

8

 9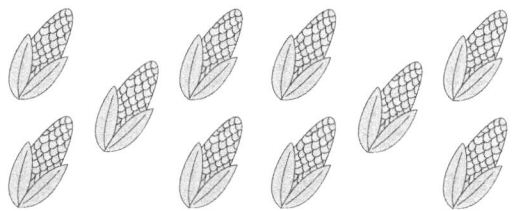

10

If you enjoyed this book, we believe you might as well like the rest of our collection of kids and adults coloring and activity books.

Visit our Author page and choose your next adventure.

Thank you for choosing

The Mus
Well-Being Institute

Made in the USA
Middletown, DE
12 September 2021